FLOWERS OF ANTI-MARTYRDOM

FLOWERS OF ANTI-MARTYRDOM

DORIAN GEISLER

McSWEENEY'S
POETRY SERIES

MCSWEENEY'S
SAN FRANCISCO

Copyright © 2017 Dorian Geisler

Cover illustration by Armando Veve

The McSweeney's Poetry Series is edited by Dominic Luxford and Jesse Nathan.

The editors wish to thank assistant editor Rachel Z. Arndt, editorial
interns Maura Reilly-Ulmanek, Waylon Elder, Megan Freshley,
Tikva Hecht, and Linnea Ogden, and copyeditor Kim Gooden.

McSweeney's and colophon are registered trademarks of McSweeney's,
a privately held company with wildly fluctuating resources.

Printed in the United States.

ISBN 978-1-944211-27-1

2 4 6 8 10 9 7 5 3 1

www.mcsweeneys.net

for Jim and Vicki Longley

CONTENTS

POEM

A poor person felt sorry for himself for being poor. Then he got angry. And then he broke things. And then he went to prison.

In prison curious things happened. Magical things. He met a man named John with a curious nose, but the nose's shape was irrelevant. Many things were irrelevant, it turned out.

The nose was operational (with John everything was 'operational'—he was an operations manager—or maybe an operations analyst—or a director of operations—whatever, it didn't matter—did it?). Anyway, he was in prison.

The prison was operational. John too was operational. Everything was operational, it turned out, and he didn't have to look out a window to realize this.

POEM

Leopard-skin print and an absence of irony overlapped: Mikhaila
stepped into the room.

The room was filled with light bulbs. It was a light bulb store.

Mikhaila was uninterested in light bulbs or their purchase. She
went straight to the back, where Deron was reading about
imprisoned celebrities.

He was also reading about prisons. He was also reading about
people. This is inevitable when you are reading about imprisoned
celebrities.

Mikhaila went straight to the back and hit Deron on the left side
of his face. She did this with her leopard-print purse.

POEM

The one-legged blues singer sat in the passenger side of the
broken car. It was a Cadillac. It had no door, and he sat facing
out, his foot resting on the sand/mud, and his shoulders hunched
underneath the top of the door frame.

It was raining. Miranda ran across the street splashing mud. She
carried an umbrella-shaped umbrella and a glass of mango juice.

She stopped facing Daquan. The rain fell on her umbrella-shaped
umbrella. It did not fall into the mango juice.

POEM

'You should have to have licenses to use certain words,' she said at George's. 'What do you mean,' I said. She paused.

'What I mean is … abstraction is nefarious. Take *death*. I can use the word *death* without having an experience of it, personally, and somebody else can use it who's seen her husband die.' 'So. That's democratic.' 'It's misleading.'

'So we should have licenses?' 'No, we shouldn't have licenses. What there should be is a suffix that means "and I have experienced this personally." And you could add it to a word like death, or heartbreak, or jury duty—anything.'

'What would you want the suffix to be?' 'I don't know. –uck. Death-uck, tragedy-uck.'

'Childbirth-uck.'

'Boredom-uck.'

'U2 concert-uck.'

'Whatever.'

POEM

Structures. We live in some. So does Winona.

Winona is very similar to us. When Winona gave birth to a child, she named it Jefferson and was filled with love.

She loved Jefferson so much. It felt like something was overflowing. But there was only so much that a mother could do (unless you count not doing something as doing something— which I don't) out of love.

Winona: 'There must be a name for that portion of feeling that is in excess of possible action; there must be a name for that feeling that just stays in your blood and burns.'

—This was in 1998.

POEM

Obligations were not fun. Serial killers and Nazis were
interesting. Things were getting hotter, generally, when Maurice
came over.

Maurice didn't like masks. But he was very good with children.
Children can be relied upon to 'sniff out,' if you will, certain
types of people.

Maurice was indeed sniffed out. It seemed there was something
that radiated from him, and children came as if drawn by a sixth
sense.

Masks depend on the sense of vision, and the availability of
vision-blocking materials—i.e., opaque.

To hear Maurice talk at night, after the children were asleep, was
to see (is *see* the right word?) a world inhabited by invisible
things.

POEM

'When you try to solve a math problem and fail, when you try to stop loving somebody and fail, when you try to stop eating a piece of triple chocolate cake and are failing, or you are trying to be kind and you end up being irritated—in all those cases you reach a limit. An end. Of your personality. Your identity.'

'Yeah but I reach an end when I jump and I can only jump so high.' He touched his right bicep. The new tattoo itched—you could tell.

'True. All I'm saying is that you illuminate a sort of mystical space—negatively, the way a sculptor carves a face out of marble—when you completely, utterly fail. You reveal the edges of a human capacity. And what is beyond your poor, human capacity? How can you tell?'

'Right. That's a very pretty thought. But it doesn't help me with the death of my grandmother.'

POEM

Once there was this man who thought he was depressed because he didn't care about the same shit everyone around him did.

Entertainment spectacles, home décors, historical figures—

Cute weeknight activities, life trajectories, shapes—

Variations of the noodle, religious rituals, standards of celebrity behavior—

Mike didn't care about the same ones that the humans within twenty-five miles of him cared about. In fact, he didn't *like* the same ones. Yes, the ones that were liked were different.

Something needed to be done.

POEM

It is difficult to estimate the number of dollars that the image of a panda has elicited from kind, unreflective people.

Kind, unreflective people are a weapon in the hands of

_____.

Kind, unreflective people aren't a weapon!

Larry the person I will not define through his profession puts coffee in his cereal's milk every morning before commuting (listening to NPR—which he really loves—as he will tell you) to a large building in which advertising is created.

Kindness is good.

POEM

They checked all over her body every morning at nine. But, Sloan realized, they never checked her tongue.

Her tongue was a place where she could cut without being discovered. But what to cut it with?

Unfortunately it was only Becky who didn't check her tongue, Sloan realized later. When Deandra was the one who checked her all over, Deandra checked her everywhere inside, also.

Rigor for Deandra, surrender for Sloan.

POEM

Oscar could stroll through a sculpture garden with a
sledgehammer, look at the *Mona Lisa* with a can of spray paint,
or sit in a missile silo for a thousand hours and not press a
button. (In fact, that is his job.)

As a human, one might be envious of Oscar. But where will envy
get you?

An author might be tempted to split the earth on either side of
Oscar. Is Oscar afraid of heights? Will a cavernous ravine finally
spawn some feeling of self-destructiveness from Oscar?

Or maybe dangle beautiful women from the ceiling? (Oscar is
married—and authors control what dangles from the ceiling.) Or
maybe offer him power—power which he could use for good,
but which he would have to procure illegally (a classic
temptation scenario)?

But let me just say: Oscar is untouchable. Authors who try to
mess with Oscar are only envious.

POEM

Fred was a happy motherfucker. Nothing else you could say.
People talked about genetic disposition, about parenting, about
luck. But what could you say?

It wasn't as if Fred never encountered difficulties in life.
Someone he loved died in a car accident, not an unknown
occurrence in these United States.

At the funeral, Fred was sad. Very, very sad—*grief* was
definitely the appropriate word for what Fred was feeling at that
time.

But still, everyone was sure that Fred would bounce back, that
his grief was 'healthy.'

Thinking about Fred's grief now (for those of us who don't
know Fred) is like looking at a diamond, in a lawn chair on top
of a mine.

POEM

They were all dancing in the all-white room, each differently,
each wearing his or her own set of headphones, each listening to
different music. Jody took off her headphones, and looked at
Jeremy. 'What's your name?'

—She had nearly yelled, but the room was almost totally silent.
She looked at all the slippered feet moving and shuffling all
around, and just behind Jeremy.

'Jeremy,' Jeremy said. He reached out his hand and smiled.

'Jody.'

POEM

Danger was correlated with authenticity. So was not thinking.

The past was correlated with authenticity, but nostalgia sat like a giant frog on the road to it.

Poverty was correlated with authenticity, but really poverty was conceptualized as a conglomerate of danger, the past, and an inability to think, and plus (to many) 'voluntary poverty' seemed either paradoxical, oxymoronic, or just moronic.

'Flirty,' Dr. Mapaulason said. 'Authenticity is a flirty thing.'

'But I don't want authenticity to be flirty,' said Ernie.

POEM

And she closed the book called *Like a Pain Fish in Pain Music*
and looked at the screen. On the screen was a background of
beautiful trees bunched together to suggest the depth of a wood.

She remembered X, she remembered Y, and then a message
appeared on her screen:

'You are the _____ of life-like-ness.'

POEM

Solomon found his attention span shortening. This was bad.
However, because of the term *attention span*'s commonness in
modern parlance, the 'shortening of his attention span' was
easily visualizable, despite its abstract nature.

Because, Solomon had trouble doing shit that took awhile.

Solomon met Nancy, though, and boy could he pay some
attention. It was either that he had more attention with which to
'pay,' or else a greater percentage of his attention was payable.

Neither could tell. This one woman wrote 'Attention is the
natural prayer of the soul.' She apparently lived before
consumerist rhetoric.

Now we can say (in praise of attention) 'Attention is natural
MONEY.'

POEM

There was a kind, fairly unoriginal person who loved his family very much. His name was Falafadon.

He went to work, and came back, and when he came back he loved his family, and this loving of his family took many forms—all of which felt great to be on the receiving end of, according to his family.

He didn't have that kind of love that really is love, but that doesn't feel that great to be on the receiving end of.

His family was grateful, though their gratitude was for the fact that Falafadon loved them, not for the fact that Falafodon's love felt good to receive.

As to whether or not his family was grateful, or appropriately so, one might say 'Falafadon—honestly—didn't give a fuck.'

Still, it is hard to speak for someone else's unconscious apathy (plus, there are many types of apathy/irrelevance—).

Try it!

POEM

'Did you see the boy?'

'Well—I didn't see all of him.'

'What did you see?'

'I saw two feet, small feet, like the feet of a boy. And I saw his—
'bottom,' I guess you would say. And I saw the bottom of his
elbows. Like he was huddled in a ball, but I could see only the
bottom of the ball, underneath the stall.'

Peggy wasn't a real policeman. Policewoman. But still, Han felt
like he should answer her questions.

Later (at home) when Han went to the freezer, his mind
elsewhere, he picked up the ice tray and moved his hands, as if
to pop ice out of it. But—there was no ice in the tray.

Han looked down at the tray surprised. Was he thinking of the
boy? Of Peggy?

He looked over to the empty glass on the counter. Something
was missing. Something that running water could fix.

POEM

There once was a man who held human action to a particular standard. 'Where did you get that standard?' Skylar asked. The man answered her.

Ten million people thought they would be raised from the dead, later. It was a big deal. Alan was friends with some of them.

There was a war 'on.' Paul Simon sang a song about being in love: 'Everyone knows you're blown apart' (because 'being in love is like having a window in your heart').

Alan moved from place to place. He bought and sold things. The year was 1987.

POEM

'There isn't ingratitude, there's just "ghost gratitude"—like for the curing of polio. It's not that we're ungrateful. It's that you have to catch the "ghost gratitude," and for this you need a certain kind of net.'

Daniel would say anything to sleep with a woman. He liked sex like a puppy likes bacon.

He was once in this situation: holding a paper cup of coffee (already cold), on crutches, in front a bathroom door outside a Chevron somewhere in Wyoming.

It was with difficulty that he opened the bathroom door. As he was peeing in the urinal, he thought about Becky. Where was she now?

Twenty years later, his leg was healed—and he was married to Sandra. Sandra of the photographic memory.

Sandra of the photographic memory, impeccable integrity, and extreme forthrightness. He knew then that the photographic memory of a spouse is the closest thing to an avenging angel—at least in marriages that might be called 'imperfect.'

Of course, Sandra didn't believe in angels.

POEM

She was in charge of casting *Revenge of the Archetypes.* But she was always distracted. She chewed on dry spaghetti because she was nervous, and ate cooked spaghetti when she was home. She was trying to save money.

She was also trying to do other things. The fact that her sister was on trial for the large-scale counterfeiting of small bills bothered her, but so did this: Craig was single. 'Craig was single Craig was single Craig was single!'—she was trying not to think of it.

She was interviewing an old man for the role of Old Man, sitting in a high director's chair, an empty box of spaghetti by her side. And in walked Craig.

Craig!

POEM

Some people were sad. Other people were dead. But there was a
sense that the dead people didn't count.

And really, they didn't. Except in the count of dead people.

Anyway, let us begin with Eduardo. Why not? Eduardo is a good
person.

So here Eduardo is, being good, in … Charlotte. But there are so
many sad people!

Maybe we should write about one of the sad people. 'But what if
 they're not interestingly sad?' 'I don't know, well fuck, we'll
just be uninteresting then? I don't know.'

So let us begin with a different Eduardo then. Let us write a book
of poems called *A Different Eduardo* and let us pass it out to
Eduardos and non-Eduardos alike.

But let us not forget other things, either.

POEM

Karma entered the slang of thousands of the sons and daughters
of the middle class.

Karma didn't mind—being in the slang of the middle class.
Karma was like a secret agent, and a secret agent doesn't mind
where he or she is.

We know this. But Karma doesn't care if we know. He is like a
secret agent—and a secret agent is unfazed by other people's
knowledge.

There Karma is, waiting in American brains, like a secret agent
in a desert's tunnels.

The problem with secret agents is, they are real.

POEM

'When you see a white person, go up to them and say 'Buy for me bread.' Do it quickly, but not too quickly. If you do it too quickly, the white person will be afraid of you.'

'Yes, the white person will be afraid of you.'

'No, you do not want bread. If they buy bread for you, that is fine.'

'Bring it back to me, too.'

POEM

Tomás's failed escapist novel was exactly as boring as everyday
life. Eloise was a model with legs four inches longer than her
torso. They met by chance in a Taco Bell, in the year 2010.

Tomás's failed escapist novel was a success in another way,
others had said, and so, if we may be as vague as to use the word
'success,' Tomás had success. Eloise didn't just have long legs.

Their meeting in the Taco Bell was the meeting of two confident,
 successful people, each keenly aware of the discipline necessary
to succeed in their respective professions.

Eloise seemed to have the upper hand, as she seemed to always,
in her dealing with a certain gender that also had a certain sexual
orientation, which Tomás was and did have, respectively.

There were chalupas.

Eloise could empathize with a photographed chalupa.

Tomás could empathize with a photographed chalupa
photographer.

POEM

In the labyrinth there was candy. Yes.

Jane opened a Twix. She was looking for the limits of human ability—but the good kind.

In the labyrinth (which had gray-green walls) sat a woman in a rocking chair. Jane said to her, 'I am looking for the limits of human ability.'

'Which kind?' she asked. 'The good kind,' Jane said. 'Oh. That way.' 'Thanks.'

POEM

Rafael claimed to have a boredom detector. He claimed it was in his soul. He was six.

Rafael learned about the soul from Jude last Sunday while eating a doughnut and talking about his grandfather in the basement of the Presbyterian Church on E. Washington.

When his mother told him to finish his science homework (a research project on a species of manta ray common off the shores of southern Florida) Rafael went 'Beep beep!' and then said, in a perfect monotone: 'Boredom detected.'

His mother, always a quick-witted woman, said: 'Careful, there, Rafael, or I will have to take that boredom detector away from you.'

Rafael responded: 'You can't. It's in my soul.'

POEM

Frank—a normal, overweight man in Santa Cruz.

In Santa Cruz there was much healthiness. This healthiness gathered itself in the brains and bodies of the inhabitants of Santa Cruz, and this healthiness gathered further inhabitants to Santa Cruz, who themselves brought with them further healthiness, which had been gathered into their own brains and bodies.

The healthiness began to reach proportions that could be labeled 'monstrous.' But that was when the boredom came.

The boredom came like a slow-motion metaphysical-existential hurricane. It lodged itself in the brains and bodies of the inhabitants of Santa Cruz, who themselves felt helpless, in a metaphysical-existential way.

Yes, boredom came into Santa Cruz like a God, like the offspring of (or wreaked devastation from) two monsters taken at random from an anthology of pre-Christian mythology.

People stopped jogging. People stopped eating banana crisps. People stopped meditating in a secular context. People ceased spiritually connecting to nature alone and in small groups.

And this—all as Frank was just getting into it! He was still out of shape, but he was jogging. He had just started meditating. He had a camping trip scheduled. What was he going to do?

POEM

All the things that might happen, leading up to the utterance
'Welcome to Florida.'

POEM

Jill resembled exactly the stereotype of her ethnic group. Her
realness was like a little kid hiding behind a tree in a game.

Jill had the capacity to amaze intellectuals. Intellectuals had the
capacity to generate stereotypes. An intellectual's assumptions
were like a slipper, and Jill was like Cinderella.

You just read the story of Cinderella, except that Cinderella was
Jill. And other things were different, also.

POEM

From the moving car the bullet penetrated the window, and then the lava lamp, and then Carl's shoulder. Sheila screamed.

She put down the navy-blue thermos that contained Campbell's Chicken Noodle Soup and got out of her rocking chair. She yelled 'Blake! Get a towel! We need to bandage Carl's wound!'

Blake knew the towels were at the laundry. So he went into Casy's room, rummaged around in the chest of drawers (he hardly ever went into Casy's room) and got out a Pampers Baby-Dry Diaper, size 3, from the third drawer. Then he rushed back to the living room.

Sheila put the diaper on Carl's shoulder. Carl didn't appear to notice. He was looking at the lava lamp, which was now shattered, and he seemed very sad.

POEM

'Having a terminal illness simplifies things,' he thought.
Looking up at the ceiling, he could see only darkness. 'It's just
me and you, now,' he said (addressing the darkness). And: 'I'm
alone.'

But that was false. Martha poked Rob in the ribcage: 'Are you
having a little self-pity party in there?'

'Where?' 'In your brain.' 'No.' 'Yes you are.' 'No, I'm not.'
'Yes, you *are*.' 'No, I'm *not*.'

'I know when there's a party I haven't been invited to,' she said.
And kissed him on the mouth.

POEM

A person who liked difficult things was Sim. Sim loved a person.
He loved that person very much, and that person was enough,
'period.'

The problem then seemed that on some nefarious level, enough-
ness was not what Sim wanted. Or maybe there was some other
problem, like that he was afraid. Or maybe he had just made a
mistake.

But, after some events, Sim and that person were no longer
together. And so the enough-ness was gone.

Gone enough-ness was very difficult.

'So many difficult things,' thought Sim.

And that is when he saw something new: a new emotional
landscape, a new sort of place.

The place was defined by a certain type of pain.

The pain was interesting, but not importantly so. A main feature
of the place was its density, the sheer quantity of people inside of
it.

POEM

Counterfactuals haunted some brains. 'If there hadn't been an earthquake, Jamilla would have been a doctor.' Et cetera.

A dart hit a dartboard. 'If Kaila had called me, I would have left my wife, and my three children, and gone with her wherever she wanted,' said a man (who then took a sip of his beer).

A friend of that man said, 'But she didn't, and you didn't,' and he, too, took a sip of his beer.

And the dart game progressed. Somebody mentioned the time. Somebody drove somebody else home, and somebody slept with somebody else.

Other things happened, and some didn't. A drunken man took off his shirt, and said (to the sky) 'Look who won the lottery of possibility—.'

POEM

'There is the sound of one machete being sharpened on the sidewalk, and there is the sound of fifty machetes being sharpened on the sidewalk,' he said, blowing out a cloud of smoke, and placing the five side of a domino next to another five side.

John nodded: right. Jerry leaned back in his chair. He called Rufus, who came running over the muddy yard, muddy.

POEM

A spermatozoa touches an egg in the uterus of a thirteen-year-old, at the same time a particular flower blooms.

It is like switching on a light, in a room with no windows, at sunrise.

POEM

Falling leaves were beautiful to people regardless of their culture of origin. Falling leaves were described beautifully in many books.

And that was good.

Sofy liked reading. She liked her dog, Ho Chi Minh, who was white, also. Sometimes it rained and Sofy would be reading a book in her bed with Hochi (what she called Ho Chi Minh when feeling affectionate towards him, which was always, more or less) and she would have only the bedside light on, and she would say nothing really, but be generally appreciative.

Some very fortunate people interpret their moral obligation to be this: appreciation. Sofy was not one of these. She was just appreciative.

POEM

I was told to write a story about a rapper in the desert. So I wrote this.

There once was a rapper named Seel. He said he didn't give a fuck. His ability to posture in a pathological yet (to be fair) masculine way was based, parasitically, on the type of danger that he faced on a daily basis, which was (of course) the danger of sudden death by gunshot—predominately. However, Steel was unprepared to face a danger different in kind, the danger of a very long, slow, painful path towards a death that may or may not come, as when one is stranded alone in an enormous desert with some (but not a great deal of) water, and with only a local government searching for you, and that only halfheartedly and incompetently, by foot and camel.

The rapper named Seel was transported to such a desert situation by a mildly sadistic writer, and had many existential revelations before being rescued by a man named Saul, on a camel.

Later, he continued to live.

POEM

An author created a microcosm of poetic justice. It was small
and petty, but, like a pet iguana, it gave him a curious pleasure.

POEM

Coolness was very cool, but was it an obstacle to something else?

Hilary wasn't sure. Often, she felt, she would be close to sensing something else, something shall we say 'deeper,' but every time, right then, something cool would happen.

And sometimes that thing that happened was very cool. She had met various celebrities, for example, while on the verge of religious experience.

She felt like she was being tested, or tempted.

The cultural model for temptation at that time was a chocolate cake. Often these cakes were named for something relating to sin or temptation.

The choice between feeling sexy and having a sugar high was like two identical twins fighting for the same magenta jumpsuit.

Hilary kept winning gift certificates.

POEM

Johnny thought he was magical. And maybe he was. When he picked up a basketball, he had the look in his eye as if it would go in the net.

Statistics were un-fuck-witable, however.

Statistics were un-fuck-witable, but Johnny knew this. Johnny was sharp. Even if he wasn't magical, you at least had to concede his considerable sharpness.

Either considerably sharp or magical, Johnny walked around and talked to people, and some people were very surprised by him. Some people took to him very strongly.

Still, some people were bored.

Yet still—one person fell in love with him. (It was difficult to deny this falling contained a magical element.) Aristotle says: *Making one shoe doesn't make you a cobbler.*

But Johnny wasn't a cobbler, was he?

POEM

Emilia said 'mercy' in the grocery store. Then she said mercy in
the post office. Then she said mercy in the car. Then she said
mercy in her house and again in the street outside of her house
next to the sidewalk.

She said mercy in other places, too. She said it at different
volumes and in a variety of different ways.

POEM

The policeman looked at the man in custody over the
interrogation table.

'Self— ... self— ... self— ...' The man was making a small
gesture with his right wrist, as if miming the movements (in
miniature) of whipping himself.

'*Flagellation*,' the policeman said. 'Yes, self-*flagellation*,' the
man behind the table said. 'Thank you. Sometime I have trouble
with words.'

A window washer, Vivek, days after being released from jail,
was again more than forty stories above the streets of Chicago,
cleaning.

He could see inside.

Words: they fail window washers, sometimes.

POEM

'The iguanodon is distinguished by its horned thumb.' The tour guide paused to give his audience time to absorb this statement. Then he moved on.

Next to the under-water display, he said: 'The plesiosaur was the top ocean predator of the Cretaceous. It is also known as the "water demon." When it was discovered, people said it resembled a snake threaded through the shell of a turtle. Although it has no shell, and is far larger than any snake or turtle.'

William looked up at the enormous skeleton. 'The plesiosaur is distinguished from other marine predators of the Mesozoic and early Cretaceous by the length of its neck.'

Outside, in the snowstorm (of 1952), the heartbroken father told his son, 'Don't confuse method of identification with essence.'

POEM

There was sunlight, black coffee, the image of a woman's hair in Jack's eyes, the transfigured image of a woman's hair in Jack's brain, windows, and other pretty things. It was very nice.

Jack, however, was a biological product of evolution, and as such, unpredictable. He had different parts.

Different parts that were different in their doing of different things. Function was hazy, and a biological product of evolution.

The situation was tense.

Imagine: a randomly selected three-year-old magically transported into a giant cake.

POEM

Jared the fat ambulance driver played the clarinet, and this he did very well. He met his first wife in a makeshift bomb shelter in San Francisco, their eyes meeting as they huddled in the fetal position, scared to death underneath a ping-pong table in the basement of the North Beach Y.

Romance ensued. It was on her (his first wife's) suggestion that he take an EMT class, which he did, and which later led to his job as an ambulance driver.

Fear, love, corpulence, ambulance driving—Jared's life was almost full (or so he thought). And then he started to play the clarinet.

POEM

'The twentieth century thinks it's cut off Job's balls. But Job's
scrotum thinks the twentieth century is small.'

It was unclear what Dave's job was, but it appeared that he was
some sort of nonprofit consultant, often working for charities or
peace organizations abroad.

He liked to tell the story of the time when he was in a Jacuzzi in
Maimana, with an Afghan warlord and seven of his men:

'I was sweating. I felt like I was sitting in a bowl of eels. The jets
of hot water, combined with the number of men in the Jacuzzi—
everywhere in that water there were various limbs (of various
types), moving slightly back and forth—back and forth—like
eels!'

POEM

Free time was there. Kyle was there. Kyle took some
responsibility and placed it on free time. Free time was okay.

People liked free time. Kyle watched bobsledding. Free time was
filled with music.

Four humans made inertia and physical limitation into an
exhilarating experience, which was appreciated by Kyle,
approximately two hundred times.

He started a band. It was called Kyle and the Riders of Inertia
(later Inertia Riderz).

He entered a Vancouver stage (followed by his three bandmates),
wearing a helmet and dancing slightly, as if careening down an
icy tube.

POEM

'Self-loathing: *Borrrrrrrrrrrring.*' Jules gave Adam back his
stack of poems and took a bite of an apple. And then shrugged.

Adam went home, depressed, but full of motivation. He sat down
in the kitchen with his laptop. He started to write.

But then he checked his email. And then he checked his other
email. Then Clio and he began talking about poetry on Gchat.

At 5:47 PM Clio sent a message: '"To write poetry after
Auschwitz is barbaric"—Adorno.' (The sun was going down.)

Adam poured himself his fifth cup of coffee. He typed 'Fuck the
crimes, now. I'm writing rhymes, now' and then he typed '—
Biggie.'

The small cactus Jules kept on his desk—just to project emotions
onto—seemed pleased.

POEM

Prayer for the Economic Development of Ecuador, line seventy-seven: 'Grant us patience, Lord, grant us the strength to deal with our temporary weaknesses.'

That is only one of the prayers for the economic development of Ecuador. There is also a second one. Its seventy-seventh line reads: 'And thank you for the bus lines, which have enabled so many of us to see friends and family more easily ...'

POEM

I fought the law. Law won.

POEM

There is only so much the entrance of a celebrity with a bullhorn yelling 'Care, motherfuckers!' can do for an unmotivated classroom. Of course, Dale (the teacher) knew this.

He used it as ammunition for his 2003 book *The Failure of Irreverence: Why We Are Treading Water in American Culture and How We Can Learn to Swim*. (He used to be an Olympic swimmer. Or nearly one.)

At a panel in Milwaukee during the 2011-2012 NBA lockout season, a Rabbi asked Dale about his experience as a swimmer, about what that had taught him about hard work, perseverance, etc. (Many of the Rabbi's congregation were in attendance.)

'Hard work is hard work,' Dale had said, drawing laughs. But for some reason—who can say where some emotions come from?— he felt sad that day, so he took a sip of water, and added: 'The will of God is the will of God.'

POEM

Bach, Goldberg Variations. In the backseat, Akhil looked out the window: Connecticut passing them by.

He fell asleep and when he woke up, his uncle, in the seat next to him, was peeling an orange. Krishna's hands shook almost violently—he had a tremor—but he peeled the orange very carefully, removing large sections of peel at a time.

The smell of oranges filled the Honda. The Goldberg Variations played.

Sergei, though driving, looked back at his brother and his son. Love—and possession (belonging?)—filled his heart.

He had to say to himself, his eyes back on the road: 'It is not *mine*. I am not entitled to it. It is like the next twenty years of my life—I would be lucky to have them.'

POEM

'Don't play with me, I ain't a video game—' the lyrics came through Mike the butcher's headphones as he looked through the window on the way to the china shop, the bus lurching back and forth (as only over-filled buses do), barely shifting the crowds of teenagers that were standing and laughing, clinging to the railings.

'I ain't no video game' he repeated as he got out at Astor and Park, turned off his iPod, and opened the glass door that led into the china shop.

In the china shop Mike saw china. (He also heard the bell above the glass door ring.) But what drew his attention (dramatically) was a small golden bull, with a note pasted on its head: 'Don't make the comment about me being in a china shop!'

Mike's brow furrowed. The young man behind the counter beamed.

Everywhere there were vessels that could break.

POEM

Things got repetitive. And when people said that, they meant
things were boring. And the word *things* was a placeholder,
really. What they meant was 'it was boring,' as in 'it was
raining.'

Here and there, though, were nuggets of not-boring-ness. People
filmed these nuggets and put them onto the television, if they
could, in so doing creating greater nugget-access.

The strange thing was, some people *were* the nuggets!

The people that were the nuggets were often called entertainers
or comedians or interesting people, and if you encountered one
you would probably try to make him/her/it your friend.

Some people say that I am resentful of the fact that people need
to have attributes other than (and additional to) personhood, in
order for other persons to care about them.

Other people say that I fail to understand the existential situation
in which people find themselves. Their line of reasoning
(roughly) is: You're going to die! Go get some of those nuggets!

POEM

Human diversity included Julia. Julia had attributes that were different from other attributes that other people had.

POEM

The prayer of St. Francis went, 'Lord, make me an instrument …'

The people who already felt like instruments didn't use it, generally. Except Flo. Flo knew that she felt comfortable as an instrument: cooking for other people, caring for other people. She was one of the type that always dated people who were always not good to the people they dated.

She never cooked for herself, and never bought nice things for herself.

Mike was a person who was concerned with cleanliness of different types. A perfectionist. He was one of the type who would put a spoiler on a Volvo, but not drive it because of emissions.

Flo would cook spaghetti for Mike. The kitchen would fill with steam. After much negotiation, they agreed that Flo would say the prayer with the following additions:

> Lord, make me an instrument of your peace,
> *make me more than an instrument of your peace,*
> where there is hatred, let me sow love;
> *let me receive love, and believe that I deserve it*
>
> where there is injury, pardon;
> *let me receive pardon, and believe that I deserve it*
> where there is doubt, faith;
> *let me receive faith, and believe that I deserve it …*

POEM

He finished painting *The Statistician's Kiss*. Then he left the studio. In the bathroom, he thought 'Still—still unable to piss. Forty-seven years old.' He shook his head and stared at the paint on his hands.

'Oh what a rebuke a functional toilet is to an old man, to an old, hard-drinking man like you, Sonny.'

Sonny turned around: It was him. His enemy—the arch-pragmatist, the Arch-Pragmatist himself—standing in the doorway of the public restroom in the old office building.

'What are you doing here?'

The arch-pragmatist just looked at him, judging. And Sonny could only think of his daughter, the woman to whom he had given yellow flowers once, in so uncomplicated a fashion, so meteorically unsuccessfully.

'I just wanted you to know that I am the gear in the center of the world, the human world, and I judge you, and I will always judge you. Always.'

Sonny smiled. To be spoken to by the arch-pragmatist was a great validation. There must have been something of use.

POEM

Some things were so beautiful they inspired sentiments that were
described as religious by people who did not quote believe
unquote in any particular religion.

Some religious people thought these people were weak-minded
hypocrites, but others were very understanding and even very
supportive. Guess which group Yolanda belonged to.

Wrong. Yolanda was incapable of experiencing beauty from a
very young age, but literally didn't know what she was missing.
Also she was colorblind. She couldn't see blue.

But Yolanda was full of redeeming attributes (redeeming—
assuming one thinks that Yolanda needs to be redeemed. I don't.
Wait … do you?).

Anyway, here is Yolanda in a telephone booth. As you might
expect, Yolanda is overweight and wearing yellow. It is an
awkward scene. She looks like a banana, but a banana that (until
recently) had been contained in a secret, invisible shell—and
then suddenly that shell had been revealed (!)—and the revealed
shell was a rectangular prism and partially translucent.

POEM

He couldn't wait to get home to Delilah, whose legs were
magical, whose face was magical, whose every movement—Ivan
thought—was magical.

He could just see her, legs crossed, sitting on the edge of the bed
(the mattress ever so slightly weighed down) and whenever she
got excited or laughed, the bed bouncing just a little, a half-
smoked cigarette in her right hand.

Delilah was working on a screenplay about a serial killer (or
killers—it wasn't clear to the audience) who murdered television
talk show hosts and anchormen using a large knife. The victims
were always found wearing terracotta masks. Each mask had a
front that was elliptical, smooth, and crudely painted gray: 'It was
as if,' the lead detective was to say in scene 3, 'their faces
had been turned off.'

POEM

A sociologist finds a lottery ticket in the pocket of a man
recently struck by lightning. The swings are empty. No one else
is in the park.

She steps over his legs. Of course, at first she doesn't know he is
dead (or that his pocket contains a lottery ticket, or that he was
struck by lightning)—she is thinking only of Yaneke, her
nephew, fifteen years old, and living with her sister in Seattle.

She almost trips over him, in fact. 'Amazing how well a corpse
can blend in to low-lying bushes,' she thinks (or might have, had
she known then that he was dead).

After the panic and the dialing of the emergency numbers, she
sees the lottery ticket.

POEM

It was difficult to praise the traumatized woman for her ability to forget, because she forgot so easily and perfectly. It was difficult to censure the traumatized woman for her use of forgetting, because her trauma was (presumably) so traumatizing.

It was like trying to praise a craftsman for the construction of a perfectly invisible, ethereal thing.

Linda was like this.

POEM

'As if in a James Bond video game, finding a secret machine
gun: the way in which you have found "forgiveness," and have
applied it, as you have, to every visible thing that moves,
laughing as you go—from level to level, confident in what you
now call (without irony) "complete victory."'

POEM

In a certain country, X, a mystic tradition grew up based partially on the proximity and availability of the hallucinogenic plant Y.

We may call a shaman from X 'Rodman.' Rodman was born, dand dreamed of many things.

'To try to conceptualize and then describe Rodman's dreams would be quixotic and obtuse,' said an anthropologist to someone who was not listening.

But the anthropologist continued thinking about Rodman's thoughts, drinking whiskey alone, and feeling a distinctive type of loneliness, particular to Canadians.

'Don't be lonely, Carl!' we may shout at him.

POEM

Horatio liked to show 'Indians' their first movie in a movie
theater. This was in Antigua, in 1976, and there was only one
movie theater, and there was also an obscene amount of violence
all over the country. He struck a deal with a priest named Pedro
to use a bus (making it seem like an act of charity)—but of
course it was really an act of violence.

The Indians—ethnic Mayans, really—would have all sorts of
reactions while Horatio watched from the tiny illuminated
window of the projector room. Some of these people (all ages)
were afraid, others fascinated, others bored (as if somehow
immune to it), while others wandered around, started fights, and
others fell asleep.

He could have fallen in love in this way, watching a woman's
frightened face from above while she stared unknowingly at the
rather enormous movie screen, showing pictures of cowboys or
well-dressed men in well-trimmed suits with beautiful women in
their arms.

It was probably just a matter of time, but the theater (owned by
Horatio) closed in 1978. Cheryl met him in 1984 and he was
already blind.

POEM

'Is that a baby at the bar?' A blonde woman had pulled up her Ramones t-shirt and was nursing a baby. Her right hand was at rest next to a tall glass of light-colored beer, and she was looking intently at the man across the table. Her left arm held the baby up and rocked him (her?) gently.

I turned back to Wayne. 'Love some of them, hate some of them—what you gotta do is read this.' And I slid a book over to him. The woman with the baby took a drink, her brow furrowed.

'*How to Empathize*? You read that shit?'

'*How to Empathize* is not a self-help book, dude,' I said, eating a mediocre onion ring.

'The onion rings are mediocre here.' '*They're onion rings.*'

The woman across the bar stood up suddenly. 'You have to understand what you are signing up for.'

The woman turned around, looking again at the man—who was wearing a baseball cap (Tigers?).

'O one, o none, o no one, o you: where did the way lead when it lead nowhere?' she said.

POEM

The editor of *The Economics of Ethics, The Ethics of Economics*
was not a martyr. Nor was he extraordinary in any way.

His favorite flower was the dandelion, and he enjoyed cooking
jambalaya with his wife, Soreya, while listening to whatever it is
Soreya wanted to listen to (often show tunes, but also opera and
the occasional Bollywood radio hit—she liked the theatrical, or
had an ear for it, it seemed).

I could describe Soreya's appearance, or her job—and in fact I
am interested in those things. But they are beside the point.

Lars had small ears and a broad forehead. He was stocky and
frequently wore blue. His face looked like—not a monkey, but
like the stuffed animal of a monkey.

POEM

It wasn't just graves that Myrtle placed flowers on. Or heads of hair. Or circular glass tables.

How can I tell you about Myrtle? Details details details—about Myrtle. But you know what? Intimacy isn't about knowing details. Is it.

You and Myrtle in a room. You asking her questions, getting to know her. Maybe you like and respect Myrtle. Maybe you don't.

But you know what? Myrtle isn't a real person. As an imaginary person, why don't you treat her like a Frito? Be as mindful of her details as you are of a Frito.

You shouldn't treat everyone like a Frito. But that is exactly how you should treat Myrtle.

POEM

Goods were produced for consumers that were both amazing and useful, and these characteristics were identifiable separately. Slam burnt his calories to control a machine that used the energy from another burnt thing to make another thing-burning machine that was both amazing and useful for us.

So, amazingness and use radiated from the large, architecturally mediocre building in which Slam worked—and, let's be honest, lived—for much of his adult life (I will not touch on Slam's childhood here).

Use. The use was used for good things like life-saving medicines, love-enabling longer lives, sacredness, seriousness, etc. Slam didn't necessarily enjoy these things directly, but other people were doing other things, and he received some benefit from that.

It was very serious, and many (really very rigorous) studies of this process were made, one of which is definitely not this.

It's not even really a study.

It's about Slam!

POEM

'Me without you like car without engine,' Carlos said into the mic, referring to Jamaila. A year later he was in jail for sexual assault of a minor.

The lyric had rhymed with 'one in a million.' Jeremiah talked to Carlos about Christ. This was in prison.

When deciding if somebody is or is not lucky (in a particular situation, X), many variables must be considered.

Tuesdays Carlos talked to Jamaila with the black phone, looking at her through the bullet-proof glass.

During Lent, his guidebook said: 'One must not become obsessed with sin. We must be careful lest our guilt become an idol ...'

POEM

'Mangos—' 'Fuck mangos, man.' 'Mangos? Fuck mangos?'
'You heard me, motherfucker. Fuck them.'

They were standing outside the can factory (maybe one should
say cannery—maybe one shouldn't say cannery) in Lima in
1973. June.

A large bird flew by—KAH! KAH!

'Fuck mangos, fuck motherfucking colorful-ass birds, fuck metal
cans full of weak-ass food, fuck a giant motherfucking factory
just sitting here—'

'You know, hating everything that not everybody can have is not
solidarity. That's pathological resentment.'

'Somebody's gotta re-read Marx.'

POEM

Importance was being allocated by a culture in which Miranda lived gloriously. She was living gloriously before, and she still is now.

Glory was here, and glory was there, and glory varied with historical epochs.

Miranda had it. She walked down the street and it radiated. You might have thought the radiation was kindness or fertility or confidence or wealth. But it wasn't.

She entered a 7-Eleven and there was a radiation battle (glory vs. unglory). But then the radiation combatants stopped fighting.

They just dropped their metaphorical swords, and Miranda's radiation soldiers and 7-Eleven's radiation soldiers just stood there, looking at each other.

Curiosity was there, and more metaphorical soldiers of glory rose up, like fake dead people after a real near-catastrophe.

POEM

The 'X', the 'not-X', the discarding of conceptual understanding:

Larry tried them all.

Larry wore a long brown coat with a tie on underneath and lived in Washington, D.C. He looked like what a superhero might look like were he to disguise himself as an ordinary person.

He took the train to work.

One day he was taking the train to work, and then the train stopped: someone had pressed the emergency brake.

It was a child with a chicken-leg in her hand. The child was Sandra. The chicken leg was approximately one-half eaten.

'Strangers collide!' Sandra yelled. It was as if she had heard the phrase on a TV show, and now was excited to repeat it at exactly the right time.

POEM

'A road was built, connecting two communities. The first
community was full of happy, healthy, competent people. The
second was full of people who were not.'

—in this way a boring yet instructive parable was written.
Johannes didn't care. Johannes wanted to play the saxophone. And
because he had a saxophone and other, more nebulous things
(like 'opportunities'), he did.

The music Johannes played on the saxophone was very
unbeautiful at first. However, as he put more and more capital of
various types into it—human and nonhuman—the music became
less and less unbeautiful, until finally it crossed that meaningful
threshold into beautiful.

On that day the number of beautiful things in Johannes's life
increased by one. However, on that day, the overall number of
beautiful things also decreased by four.

On that day there was a net loss of three beautiful things. Of
course, that is not the full story.

POEM

On the front page of *The New York Times* was a photograph of a
collage of limbs and various other body parts (of various races,
of various ages) with *IMPOTENT* in various fonts and styles
tattooed on each of them. Mae read the accompanying article out
loud to Qui, who was driving (Mae was in the passenger seat).

They were on their way to Chicago, to visit their mother, in
Qui's '99 Subaru.

When Mae read the article's reference to Matthew 18:9, 'And if
your eye causes you to sin, gouge it out … it is better to enter the
Kingdom of God with only one eye than to have two eyes and be
thrown into the fire of hell,' Qui became visibly upset.

Then he became thoughtful. 'What do you do if your eye doesn't
cause you to sin, but doesn't do a goddamn thing, either?'

POEM

Claire sat in the subway station on 116th and read the sentence
'There is only one unhappiness, and that is—NOT TO BE ONE
OF THE SAINTS'—as trains passed her going both ways,
without stopping.

She was probably going to be late. She had forgotten to buy the
asparagus. Ryan wouldn't mind, but he would also enjoy not
minding too much.

She could make them get into a fight, by feigning self-loathing
again.

To feel normal, to be allocated normal levels of forgiveness, to
have that forgiveness feel normal, to have normalcy be enough
…

If she had to pray with only one word, she thought—getting on
the train—it would be *enough*.

ACKNOWLEDGMENTS

Grateful acknowledgments to the following journals, in
which some of these poems first appeared: *LVNG*, the *Believer*,
Ampersand Review, and the *Alarmist*.

Dominic Luxford and Jesse Nathan chose this manuscript to
make a book out of, when really they could have chosen a lot
of others. I'm grateful for that. Also, they helped make the book
good. In a fun way.

A lot of people taught me about writing in a classroom. I am
grateful to those people, too.

There are many people that I would like to include in this
section because I think they would appreciate being included in
this section. Not only that, but they deserve to be in this section!
Thank you. You talked to me about writing:

Jeff Cravens, Dash Davidson, Eric Dryden, Ossian Foley, Harry
Gail, Jordan Ginn, Jeremy Jacobs, Eleza Jaeger, Justin Kramon,
Jim Longley, Vicki Longley, Daniel Rozenblatt, Daphne
Rozenblatt, Emily Ruskovich, Ben Siegelman, Paul Thibodeau,
Andrew Wells, Jane Wong.

—and in all sincerity, I would like to thank Amanda Vacharat for
all her help and early edits—and my parents for their support. I
would particularly like to thank Cay Geisler, who is the reason I
read and wrote things at all. I am very grateful to her.

ABOUT THE AUTHOR

Dorian Geisler is a graduate of UC Berkeley and the Iowa Writers' Workshop. He has taught at the Millennium Art Academy and Arcadia University, and his poetry has appeared in the *Believer*, *Hayden's Ferry Review*, *LVNG*, and the *Berkeley Poetry Review*. Geisler is currently studying law at the University of Michigan.

THE McSWEENEY'S POETRY SERIES

THE McSWEENEY'S POETRY SERIES WOULD
LIKE TO THANK THE FOLLOWING DONORS FOR
THEIR INCREDIBLE SUPPORT:

Jeremy Rishel, Matt Mullenweg, Dan Grossman, Sean Healey, Alex
Ludlum, Sandy Nathan, Kirsten Zerger, Matthew Dickman, Uttam
Jain, Victor Jih, Andrea Lunsford, Joyce Carol Oates, Patricia Parker,
Phoebe Putnam, Jenni Baker, Charles Baxter, Paul Eldrenkamp,
Marshall Hayes, James Juhnke, Douglas Kearney, Daniel Khalastchi,
Oliver Kroll, Richard Lang, Julian Orenstein, Alf Prue, Atsuro Riley,
Ed Ruscha, Faisal Siddiqui, Jim Swinerton, Brian Turner, Irena
Yamboliev, Brandon Amico, Nicholson Baker, Hans Balmes, Mark
Dawson, Melinda DeJongh, Abigail Droge, Mary Dumont, Aiden Enns,
Mike Gavino, Anne Germanacos, Ray Khalastchi, Lila LaHood, Katie
Lederer, Charley Locke, Ruth Madievsky, Ander Monson, Jim Moore,
Klainie Nedoroscik, Adam O'Riordan, Sairus Patel, Nicole Ryan, Kent
Shaw, Colleen Sanders, Charlie B. Spaht, and Pauls Toutonghi

THE PUBLICATION OF THIS BOOK
WOULD NOT HAVE BEEN POSSIBLE
WITHOUT THEIR GENEROSITY.

THE
McSWEENEY'S POETRY SERIES

The McSweeney's Poetry Series is founded on the idea that good poems can come in any style or form, by poets of any age anywhere. Our goal is to publish the best, most vital work we can find, regardless of pedigree. We're after poems that move, provoke, inspire, delight—poems that tear a hole in the sky. And when we find them, we'll publish them the only way we know how: in beautiful hardbacks, with original artwork on the cover. These are books to own, books to cherish, books to loan to friends only in rare circumstances.

»»——«««

SUBSCRIPTIONS

The McSweeney's Poetry Series subscription includes our next four books for only $45—around $11 per book—delivered to your door, shipping included. You can sign up at *store.mcsweeneys.net*.

»»——«««

PREVIOUS TITLES

Remains by Jesús Castillo
"Riveting complexity and range, and capacious enough
to contain multitudes." —DEBORAH LANDAU

Whosoever Has Let a Minotaur Enter Them, or a Sonnet— by Emily Carr
"Carr explodes our understanding of ourselves and what we might
be doing here on this planet." —DARA WIER

The Abridged History of Rainfall by Jay Hopler
"By these poems, your faith will be shattered and restored, restored and
wondrously shattered again." —CRAIG MORGAN TEICHER